Stretch of Closures

CLAIRE CROWTHER

Stretch of Closures

Shearsman Books
Exeter

Published in the United Kingdom in 2007 by
Shearsman Books Ltd
58 Velwell Road
Exeter EX4 4LD

www.shearsman.com

ISBN-13 978-1-905700-18-9

ISBN-10 1-905700-18-0

Acknowledgements
Some of these poems, or earlier versions of them, have appeared in *Ambit,
The Cortland Review, Freedom Rules, Magma, New Welsh Review, Obsessed with
Pipework, PN Review, Poetry Flash* (California), *Poetry Review, Poetry Wales, Poetry
Salzburg Review, Shearsman,* and *The Times Literary Supplement.*

The publisher gratefully acknowledges financial assistance
from Arts Council England.

Contents

Untitled

Forthcoming Titles

This book is dedicated to Anna Maria and Eric

*I like a
loved one to
be apt in
the wing.*

Lorine Niedecker

Next Door Moon

Reconstructive Fortressing

They were moving about the rooms, two men.
My daughter said, I don't want to live with them.
No, no, I said, they will live here alone
if they buy our place. We will have gone.
Do you remember that large patch of green
I called the country? That's where we will be.

I've been wearing this flat for far too long.
It's dark though I've accessorised it in turquoise.
It works best when my skin is palest in winter.
In summer it makes me look tacky. I am ready
to invest in a house as well-fitted as a bra,
none of that faux leopard skin, no balconettes.

How to explain this perfectly reasonable reason?
From her Juliet balcony, she squints at the Eye,
a toy Big Ben fixed, neat, inside it.
She is going to have to give up her view.

Next Door Moon

The boat man is throwing Claire de Lune
in the bin. Tiny jackets of sound
hang on the curl of his next door moon.

Black nails. Her hair ripples like sand
when the sea has packed its big blue bag
and run. Driving home, we startled an owl.

It rushed across the motorway, ruffed up
and tabby. *The bridge of your nose will break
if you sniff at moonlight through the wall.*

Wouldn't Couldn't Weren't

The child is running on and off the doorstep. She won't
Come back when the mother calls. Or when she comes, doesn't
Stay. Puts one foot on the step. The cul-de-sac isn't
Busy but such a small breath flashing on the camber wouldn't
Necessarily alert a reversing car. Before these, there wasn't
A single dysfunctional family hereabouts. Their neighbour mightn't
Condemn it openly but panics in case . . . I'll murder you – can't
People drum up a kinder language of control? Mrs Raine couldn't
Ever have said that to her long dead son – the woman mustn't
Push the child further but has to catch her. They don't
Take more than seconds to regain the pavement and it shouldn't
Matter that the lemon squeezer in the mother's hand didn't
Hold its juice but stung both, making them yell more. Mrs Raine
        hasn't
Breathed so deeply for years through lungs she half believed weren't.

Parent

All I have to tuck around her, sleeping
  on the grass, is this
    transparent mac,

a cellophane as tough as the gravity
  that makes a child thunder
    like a pulpit.

Wyvern

They're millinery, roofs, pinned with cranes.
Or dirty sweatbands, the sweeps of concrete
topping blocks. We bang the slats,
kneeling above the Carphone Warehouse,
unroll felt like a black towel.

The boys say once I'd have been forced
to stay down there, on the pavement,
selling eggs and heart-cakes.
Wrong.

There would have been women, hammering,
smelling this smoke from a bitumen bin chimney.
The female dragons.

Me, I carry a hose of fire.
I can stand to walk the metal sky
and land on scaffolding like pigeon shit.
I steer by the brown reins of the Wharf.

Two of us roll up the material
to the beginning again, lay it out more slowly.

I flame each turn.

In the days of smocks, I'd have been drunk
from scurvy grass ale like the boys
around Wandsworth Plain, sobering up
on saloop, made of cuckoo flowers.

Pollen

O Source du Possible, alimente à jamais
Des pollens des soleils d'exils . . .
        Jules Laforgue
        (Complaint du Temps et de sa Commère L'Espace)

Broken red slats of a blind horizon
hanging
behind a rope
suspended
between an oak and a concrete post in a clearing
light up a honey-green leaf of girl
fluttering
down the line. Once, boys grasped the handgrip and
launched
into a draft of unsure sky.
Such machinery of
grabbing,
diving,
falling
to the ground once made a cloud
of men, a storm that
rushed
in from a sea. The sun has no time
left for fire. A torch
drops
spots of gold, tiny as pollen grains.
The slats are
sheered
off from the sky, worn out.
She runs beneath them while they
fly down
again and again like rare Red Wakes.

Persephone's Refusal

Coming on her drunk, death hunches over the girl lying near the
   station snack stand.
An advert flowers from the marble –Top Shop. Smells are a
   polygamy of soups,
minestrone, bouillabaisse, clam chowder.

Images of food and clothes,

she struggles to think,

they'll be all death will have of me.

Tries to read aloud,

Bright New,

Don't Miss Out.

He touches neck through hair.

Pushing away the paunch heavy with souls, she stands, walks
towards the soup-eaters and tells them stories – letters hidden in
log-piles, five sisters kissed by the same blackguard, policemen
falling off hay carts, the shooting of Canon O'Keefe in mistake
for a rabbit – while the cooks ladle today's special, Big Jack's
Split Pea, into thin cartons.

Ticket Language

Across the barrier flashing Seek Assistance,
Soda waves her special low-cost ticket.

The metal palms stay up. From a closed circuit
TV camera, local resident Stain

is spotted having trouble articulating
her ankles on six inch stilettos. The guard

reads Soda's claim in ticket language:
Valid As Advertised South Central STD

DaySave Any Ctrl Stn while
a stranger supports Stain's attempts to rebalance

a severe lateral wobble. Two guards search
for material relevant to the promotion

that issued Soda's ticket. White plastic
bats wave off fresh trains. Stain hears

her mobile, clenched against her ear,
say: Listen, we are running to time.

Investigating the Easter Issue

A featured fish leaps in the air, its frail
snow-white flesh encased in a monument
of salt then resurrected. The picture editor
described the cookery shoot: how trains shook

the assembled towers of lights behind Waterloo.
But I was interested in the serious section,
Trad Stuff, especially that box where the subs list
reader-martyrs who have died for the Word

(whatever it happened to say). A double-page spread
full-bleed picture of gorgeous Roman streets
showed the ancient marble kerbs worn
into dips. Perhaps by wagons of animals

going to circuses? We start you thinking,
the editor beamed. Flora, Lucy, Felicity.
Did they run home for orechietti first,
little pasta ears, rehearsing the final

no to sacrificed meat? Were those flashes
of exquisite clothing, the miraculous
makeovers of martyrdom, a living
sign of faith in hand-painted words?

Bookshelves

Packed with who she has set out to become.
Chasing Che, Cocaine Nights, The Crone Bag.

Designing an individual at odds with Memories
of Old Dorking, a book I once gave her.

Parvana's Journey, The Crime of Father Amaro,
Koto Mama: she is in several countries

at once, probably. Meanwhile, in Brixton,
that puddle left after the rain of adolescence,

her boyfriend reads The Art of Travel
while parenting her new self. Hard, I imagine.

Her Boyfriend

He says to the bloke   you don't know
Me, comes round   the bar,

Smashes a bottle   on his head
So he doesn't know what   drags him

Out to the street.   Out there
He shoots off   both his hands.

And he's not in jail.   What shall we
Do tonight?   I don't know, do I?

Neck Phase

My daughter is resculpting; it's the neck phase.
Her neck has lengthened. While I sleep
she fixes rings beneath her chin
or some such trick. Adulthood

should harden new bones. Like pregnancy
hers soften out of our thick shape
to a strange long. I am a woman
with no neck myself: Babushka,
the Venus of Willendorf.

She doesn't want a Baptist's head
to show to Herods on a muscley platter.
She stretches a protective scarf of language,
Lycra words round her new upright.
I remember discovering that tactic.

My mother's sunken head, in its ampleness
of flesh, watched me wrest separateness.
My neck is only a vestige of that struggle.
It takes some swallowing,
the falling back to collar.

Try! Please, to be Sorry.

I'm sorry, please, I'll try again later.
Again, a sorry try. I am later
and not pleased. I am so afraid
the person you are knows I am waiting.
The person knows I am phoning.
The phone! knows
the person I know. Don't I know anyone
else? You know that phone? It is like a person.
I am sorry it is the phone. Please wait
in. Try to be phoning. Try to know.
Or be explanatory. Have I mistaken you
for a careless person without a number
to leave? Sorry! again. Me, again.

Abscond

A girl among remaining leaves shakes her branch, above black
fishes tailing through willow roots past the indigo toe of a sock
flapping in the flow of a stream, and reaches across a fence.

I shout 'Jump.'

My shoes are pocked with mud. Roller skates flicker ball
bearings
like dynamos in my hand. Do I see more than my mind which
is sure that fledglings cry almost soundlessly from a nest, that a
marble lies hidden, glass budded in a scald of nettles inside the
paling?

Pebble-dash,

crazed now, is also there, on that old crate of a house with its
registration of us.

Stairborne

A torn piece of blue paper darts about,
hangs beside a face that
rushes

round, down the starry arms of a galaxy,
looking for gravity. Gusts of
wind

brush hair upward to a sharp bark
above a boy's accordion, a
brake.

Lost Child

Scrape the ditch that fits Hob's Moat
to Hatchford Brook. Look through oak roots,

the horse field, uphill to Elmdon.
Is she hiding behind that sky-blue Lexus?

Shout toward the airport. Planes rise
and fall as if ground were a shaking blanket.

Up there, the air hostesses smile.
Inflate your own life-jacket first.

The small original airport building stands
apart, a mother at a school gate.

Pearl was playing quietly alone.
My ear is like a shell the wind swept.

Quai des Bergues

A model, hair meticulously braided,
stamps her boot heel on two baguettes.

A flock of seagulls fight ferociously
for primacy when she will give permission

to eat. On each side of the bridge, a man
watches her. One, in a pilot's hat,

leather earflaps down, holds two leashes.
The other man, tight-fitting coat,

legs crossed, palms a tiny camera.
He shuffles, furtive, so unlike the birds.

Untethered

Echo on St Valentine's Day

I lay down half-naked.
Blue paper tore. Shoes
beat behind the locked door.

Lie on your hip; your hand
flat on your thigh. She stuck
a contact on each shoulder,

smeared gel round my breasts,
sat near me, her arms shaped
so that our bodies knit,

an enlarged plain stitch
she worked within, not dropping
once. I heard my heart murmur,

well done, well done,
wished on, wished on.
She listened to the voice

she gave my heart. It spoke
to a gallery of soap,
tissue and disinfectant.

A yellow bin lined with yellow
shone bright as my blood.

Moods

Once I had a motorway of hair,
long, black, stood up to stresses well.
You trafficked it, your fingers heavy, light.
I closed it once or twice against the terrors
you get with hair. One day, a lake of sun
drowned the usual distance between us.
Planes dipped their beaks in it.
People doffed clothes from upper bodies
in surprised respect, whistled through fingers,
eased back muscle. Terrace ends raised
exhausted faces to its shower. Games
splashed in its shallows. It sprang like balls from the rough
along the road. At noon, on TV,
it was historicised. The hottest day
since records began.

When, at four,
my cloud of hair plugged the sun,
we dried out dull.

Ah, motorways. We protest
because they seem to lace
our towns with ladders.

But I remember you climbing
towards where I shook
the last drops of sun from the top rung,
hand over hand, binding
your feet in ripples of starless rope.
How together we watched
the uncontrollable underneath of my hair.

Honeymoon

Even the rock smells its mortality,
even through millennia. Even granite
senses its exfoliation. She is

determined to see Bridal Veil Fall
but he, scared of such a steep gradient,
a cliff falling away to one side,

no fence to the path, grips any
girth, bole or boulder. Going, going,
ready or not, she shouts ahead of him.

Clouds skip flimsy dresses across
the sky. He watches out for streams, gullies,
twists his ankle tripped by swallow-holes,

stumbles over roots. Here at last
is the green lace, aqua silk,
torn, wrinkled, its slippery nature

pouring away, less like Niagara
than tears, and her, a full cast
of his own damp, uncommon faces

Sanding the Floor

Still arguing about the finish
of the old pine as it would have been
in forty-seven when Attlee flourished
here as quietly as Capone died
where you come from and when my grandmother
was born of a woman determined never to shine
who carried face tissues, filmy, pink,
impregnated with powder, we raise our masks,

cotton wet with breath, to concentrate
on the original boards, narrow, moled
with rubber, the paint, a sixties purple, burned
to warts. Yet pleased and baffled by our patience,
these long bodies of soft wood lie
still, samples dirty from trying.

Nudists

In the home of the naked, glass is queen.
A rule of sunlight on his left shoulder.
Her forearms hide a Caesarean scar

and a tied net curtain tries
to billow towards thighs that stray apart.
It serves a surprise to passers-by.

Nakedness is not the revelation
of glass. No less opaque than neighbours,
especially after dark when she loosens

the long hair of voiles. He stops talking,
notices that the window is hung with one
slant reflection of them both, framed.

Warrener

Along the row of huts, *Lazy Jays, Icarus, Gull's Way, The Shoe,* and past the shabby row of smaller sheds without verandas, hearing you spell a wish-list of Christian names, *Elizabeth, Victoria, Queenie,* each halo of letters glowing over a red or white door like the orange damp around doorknobs and hinges, hearing the sea exhale

onto my feet, drag
shingle back in
again like oxygen,
Shalysim, Slepe.

Late autumn. Only one hut open. A woman, covered in fleece, eyes closed, in a deckchair listening to a sound,

lo sciabordio,
sea biting the shore.
I choose its wet
and gentle muzzle.

Choose to conceive. What is free will for?

Let's leave the boardwalk to catch the tiny crabs immured too long in casket manors of sand. Hearing lo sciabordio, they come out of the ebb, in a froth of low water.

Postnatal

Men, composting Rose Garden, push
buggies full of tanned fragments.

Rose bushes spurt, dark red
April fledglings propped among the paths.

A baby cries, without the delicates cycle
to calm him, tumbling and stopping.

Each man throws his shovel into
a heap on a torn, fallen

advert, a model touching
an intricate buckle.

Caught by Workmen

Sometimes, like a mother,
a blackened burned building

collapses out
of its protective clothing

toward the traffic, which laughs
in another language.

Foreigners in Lecce

Home is rind-hard
so we have come here
to tarmacked marble,
angels on great walls

brought down by weather.
We look over
olive trees whose hips tilt
above October mats,

bones and joints ready
to shake down the little
fruit they carry. An outburst
of autumn birds, like rust

or falling oranges
in a courtyard. Now
something asleep in us
is blown like glass.

Fame Ancestrale

A day grafting marble to sills and steps,
pouring cement along bridges, campo to campo.

Swollen-fingered and cold, Massimo eats
cod soaked since morning in garlic

and milk with nubs of pecorino.
Polenta pots decorate the ceiling

like putti. His ancestors are famished,
stuck in a city made of the amber stone

that flakes like cheese. A white shirt hangs
like salted fish over the black canal.

Piave

The wind pulls the hair of young pines.
Above their heads, dinosaur footprints.

The mountain walls are frayed with paths
as if boots had churned the hills

with human weight: the alp is young,
its peaks not yet eroded smooth.

A woman wipes her face with a sun hat.
She was the tall child in a village

between two tors when a new dam
cracked open, emptying its lake

with a wave of water that spun cars
like fir cones. Engineers balance

predictions and economies.
Her home is slightly south of itself,

its thousand dead belled in a memorial.
In the place where every cloud stops,

you can hear the wheeze of a saw
building a ski lift for winter,

the heart murmur of Crumbly Mountain,
the whistle of a marmot to its mate.

Shine

... all in our apartments,
The world untended to, unwatched.
George Oppen (Myself I Sing)

A plasticised fabric cover on a motorbike,
petrol blue and green of peeling eucalyptus trunk,
the still water in a granite bowl in a calmly
horizontal driveway: all hang with shine.
Imagine
its subtlety, even inside my muscle where streams
of glycogen gleam as climbing dams them for sugar.
We play shine – we swap
glazed posters of Culture Clash and Rawson Democrat,
wheelie bins for calla lilies.
Now our shine,
like lesser stars has darkened, we can identify
better, things that shine, vitreous, resinous, splendent,
anything adamantine – cars like water droplets
splashed on the hot bypass, boats like tiny stones skimming
the marina, spots of tarmac lustre.
Think of us
next to these images, retinues of the sun,
as salts of silver, bromide or chloride, blackening
in light. We pause, absorbed by garden rooms, their retinas.

City of Turns

The sea rolled itself into a sweat
down our faces as if the tide
had suddenly thought of us as inlets

while radiant-crested, gorgeously-winged
dark-red and orange container crates
trembled from cranes on the dock

and a dead foal's eyes stared toward them
along a horizon striped with steel.
Ripples of sand spread to her mane,

relaxed as if from running. The dunes
hid other burials. I covered
the head with my shirt. My breasts,

salt quartz. Seagulls curfewed
an eagle. A shovel of wings packed him off
across this city of turns, the sea.

Untethered

Seabirds are making chains, clattering white beads against the neck of the steeple, each bead winged to keep it high and circling.

The red balloon rolls upright on the bank of the Elbe.

Collapses several times.

Your scalp shines as you climb in.

I feel like a loaf baking.
I cool my hand on the polished willow sill.

The balloon's throat is torched again and again.

We rise fast to the right over observers drinking Kaffee Vis a Vis on Europe's Balcony and in the Zwinge tethered to Mozart by a koto zither.

Against the Evidence

I like jostle. You and I a crowd.
Aggregate in the station yard.
In the carriage, arm along an ear,
thigh pressed to a baby's head,
Friday breath through a gap of faces.

A woman wearing long black velvet
glides through our carriage, flies the carpet
that locks feet. Arcs of air open
in front of this ghost and close behind,
fading passengers out. They don't realise.

Deva, I thought, or dea abscondita,
when she began to hang across my light,
a jalousie. It was the night you stayed.
Since then, Piera has arrived and gone
with you but speaks only to me.

I get up every morning, convinced
we'll live forever, against the evidence,
and call that happiness. I think of scientists
researching the expansion which will be
the end of our universe, not just my world,

who will recall, like that end, all ghosts
including her. But lately, she has shown
you are equally ghost in my life, the lover
without rights, appearing on my pavement,
on my flight, in my albergo.

Your hands among my papers established
their own directions and hours, as lawless
as Piera is. You have both researched me
and I shall track her down, my bracket of lies.
She skates all the way to Porto Badisco

47

and leaves us there for an hour alone,
and alone on the fleur de lis
of the hotel bedspread, mocking me
for chasing her living self yet pushing
her ghost into the drawer with the Gideon bible.

Saturday. Lemon of winter. Damp charcoal
bramble. Grey quilts of cloud. Wind tumbles
the wrapping from our ciabatta as if *future*
is the rim of a beaten country
and we've reached it. I want the ghosts

in every word to stand too close
to wheel-splash as Piera does,
to stalk low bridges like double-deckers.
We shrink, one surface after another,
flesh then soil, marble then Lecce tufa,

the local stone made of giant fossils.
Piera used it. Her work dissolved
as if it were the custard Dentoni,
the Big Teeth, moulded for crema.
Fourteen-eighty. Snow.

That cold Friday, she carved
a Passion. A down of limestone
and holm-oak fell from her adze.
Wild peacock meat screamed in the pan.
The Adriatic tore itself like veiling.

Piera thought of ground diamond,
the finest known poison. A husband's hand
smells like tufa, warm, rough,
open to the weather. She walked from town,
wearing the mail shirt he had forgotten,

to find the wet eyes of rock.
The storm tore holes in bark,
picked off boulders, ripped up frail
olive mats, plucked at boar bristle.
The soles of her shoes shouted, control us.

To find the hidden cave, his discovery,
his place to take women. Slippery.
They would clutch him while the sea spat
balls of white saliva at a cliff
that let its strata go like leaves.

Piera haunts any hint of pleasure:
the subterranean nymphaea, the bars,
stone fences where the horses waited,
the busty saints bulging from church roofs,
jacuzzi bath, neon logo pouring

apple brandy. They decay
into an abandoned industrial area
when Piera joins us. You don't see her.
You insist I imagine blacked-out windows,
broken-boned blinds, wisps of plastic.

I didn't arrange to meet a ghost,
yet there she was, in the British Library,
at Waterloo, in Caffè Nero,
watching our affair. We were her map
from that first rush-hour you pushed through

to say I was your genius, to say thanks,
to tell me dates and times I had appeared,
a sign to you that life would work again.
She had been a footnote in the book
I was writing on Puglian nymphaea.

It was you who called her out of her paper
shroud, up from my bibliography,
when you called me. Today, we drift
through Lecce alleyways, their marble sills,
past men with hair the colour of hot tarmac,

and faces that are redrafts of Caravaggio,
posters of Berlusconi out of Caesar.
She sips every glass of red you drink.
You don't even notice the mouth print.
Sunday evening. You'll go home alone.

When soft Lecce stone is cut,
the guide says, *in loro passa virtute,*
che le pregia, e che l'indura:
virtue enriches it and hardens it.
She murdered them, husband, mistress,

hauled the big rocks to fill
the natural gateway to the cave
where, she shouted to the wind, no-one
was laughing at the weather, wrapped
in down, hot as the smell of drying canvas.

Fragments of her art are buried in crypts,
her scarlets, purples. We are history.
But non-existence poses a singularity.
The end of passion is counter-intuitive.

Quarrel

Clots of snow are smashing
onto the brick.

Terrified pine horses are shaking off
a sudden intake of winter.

There's a dictionary of crystalline language.
Who doesn't know it?

Look at that magnolia. Its shoulders
are shocked into holding
the snow while it crouches by high walls.

They build hotels in Iceland with snow.

Could I go there?

Sleep alone on snow stones?

Marriage, Off Season

The car park is empty first thing
except for a young boy who leads us

to a telescope scrutinising sea.
Over a wall, down a thousand steps

to a doormat of beach. Back up,
a lane appears in a garden. To a headland,

clay slipping feet on, pretending to suck
shoes in when a storm shoots over.

A turn to a dry hamlet through fields
as homely as Warwickshire. Not talking.

Late in the day, a bus. Children and learners
on horses wave. Past locked chalets

to the car, now one of many parked
though the barrier is still raised.

Flag Waver

Take the wheel. This is a good
winter stretch of sand packed

with wet but it's friable.
His car dips, almost kneels,

perhaps to the black cave.
She tells him: The fender's stuck.

Take the wheel. She does, she
for whom a car is always breasting

a hill, always forced to fly
brakeless in front of her.

Take the wheel. Is glassed in case
the wind whips its sheet to crack

across them. The cliff turns: scoured,
hunched, petrified, hollowed,

slapped and bitten about.
So, drive. A tumble of stones

rises in front of the cave.
Her calves and arms float

in the driver's space. The rock
walks the beach, more mobile

than you'd think, a flag
of convenience for their country.

The Sentence Mender

I carry my voice out at night away from our house to West Hill junction.

There is a seat by the bus stop. Drivers pull in, in case I want to board.

I wait

alongside engines and sirens

till heels, brakes, horns, cut-off exhausts, the blue hat man, phones, wheels

have quietened,

till black sacks have been shredded by foxes and strewn at my feet and maple leaves have diminished to bronze stars on the paving stones.

Then I storm this firmament,

blare from scaffolding, against murders of windows, in the drizzle of twenty-four hour supermarkets.

At home, my husband hates the sound of me.

I work on it in the garage,

a sentence mender.

Weekend in Belgium

The Belgian teacher Charlotte Brontë loved might have called
that gannet bobbing the waves a Solan goose, Sulla Bassana, a
booby in the third dictionary sense,

my husband mentions, leaving his laptop to go out to the beach.
I press Recycle Undelete and restore an email

thinking about the Belgian teacher's wife who stitched the pieces
of English copperplate, ripped and binned by her husband.

I dream about you, the email reads. Underneath, *This E-mail and
the files transmitted with it are private and intended for the use of the
individual addressed.*

Alone,

holding the half-joined thing, she would have read the rescued
slivers. *If you are not the intended recipient, the E-mail has been sent
to you in error.*

Then, political borders were as undefined as, now, the emotional,
my husband might offer for an analysis.

I wave to him,

an old man harvesting oysters.

Firework

His balls hang over the scarred enamel
of the claw foot tub. He steps in.

She lies back, a woman who was once
risky, a coronation, a caprice

to thrill crowds, skim along the Thames,
dive, flash. She filled water with ordnance

and now the space she lets him have is packed
with old sun. The hot tap pushes

his shoulder blade, the Victorian lip of the bath
touches him, like her reddening skin.

Untitled

Martha's New Extension

A yellow digger attacks the hill, is stopped
by a jerkin belted with tools, shouldering
two by twos, dragging another to a pile
marked by an empty bottle. They listen to me,
lie, build as they like. They didn't need

to tear that wall down. Look at the hole!
Many colours of brown, stern faces
lean into the cave where a neat scarlet
ghost of Fair Isle is bringing a rake
back from behind bright orange fencing.

Like the illuminated psalter builders,
they have clambered through the alphabet
of my house all my life and I've stewed
tea so thick the spoon stands in the brew
to clear my dust out of their mouths.

Gecko's Tail

The gecko is out of bush cover. His tail
looks back. His head fixes on the pillow of soil

at the sound of a swan tackling the air.
A party of ducks stops dissipating, sleeps. Here

under full sun I'm burning in black jeans
to watch an animal that disappears into stone

stay with the shadows. The wash from an invisible boat
shakes the jetty. The gecko discovers concrete,

a tube, a maple leaf, a spilling carrier,
as though he's never lived here,

has to fight to stay. The coiled ducks start.
One flick of his olive-twig tail, a martial art.

Boom

The night you sailed on the QE2, I remember
having some kind of paranormal experience.
My bed shook trying to straighten itself.
As it turned out, the hotel had been bombed

in your birth year. I'm guessing you want Marmite
as you can't get it there. Wine on Saturdays
here. Diet beer in the week.
Your gifts have always made me laugh, the dahlia

that hums Davy Crockett, the collage
of you and all the children in a tent.
It reminded me of an Anderson shelter.
Jet Cars will meet you. I don't drive

to the airport now. If I wear a dress, it's not
to be formal. If I wear black, I always have.

Posts

i

gateless gateposts extruded
out of frontage going home
my friend C who has had a
lump biopsied needs to be
surprised by an odd though
comfortable topic to make a
turn for our uptight necks

ii

look there she says the sunny certainty
of that Cotswold stone untopped broad
footed post the word lodge carved
in Victorian letters it's
been there for over a
century the left post's
gone and a sweep of
drive the house violet
wild buddleia strokes its limbless shoulder

iii

unemployed gateposts stand
at the eleven storey flats and
Park View nursing home the
millionaire's house unfenced
council estates we park there
C climbs out quietly her body
nibbled only by men sons Dr
husband he waves from their
folly built in the thirties like a
pleasure dome rain and sun
dissect the brick a bare front
garden no grass gravelled to
two cars' width an iron portal
lettered PALACE in an echo
of pre-war wit welcomes her
to the private future of a lost

iv
domain
her home's
graceful posts
are bluish veined
delivering territory easily
through a landscape of past
values they're round she said
I've never noticed my round
gateposts repointed so
often by my husband
no gate in our time

Glide Church

Wheeled to the front for healing   I hear him speak.

Behind him purple and red choir vowels,
      dark suits of consonants.

A signer opens her gate of hands   for the deaf.

I stand in my seat to watch   his words.

She pincers them   rolls some.

Her thumb drums on a fist   each knuckle proud
                        as a vertebra.

Is there a neon   between her fingertips
      like an ice thread at sunrise?

I crane to make it out.   We wave our palms.

The signer's wrists flutter   applause.

We came to see gods   this damaged one,
      this one with the dancing horns.

Motorway Bridges

The seven a.m. news chips in and out.
A cannibal on trial. The two women
killed each week by partners are designated
a government priority. My body

is similar to how it was before
the diagnosis was made but there are words
now. The announcer is muffled by each bridge.
My wipers stick on light rain. I've tried

to glimpse my fate in the wing mirror . . . not telling
anyone. Morning unwraps a bolt
of hedge in dark lengths. Milošević can't
attend a judgement on genocide. I'd opt

out of treatment on any grounds – the nurse
holds my flinches in case I spill the chemical.
A word I'm thinking of is (irrelevant) 'henge'
because fogged concrete looks like stone.

Display on Sussex Ward

Yarrow: verdant, ravelled yarnburst,
shells of thread
cloud the emerald hills
of Vandyke and double featherstitch,
whipped web and long-armed feather.

I reach out. A man points to a notice:
'Don't touch.'
The paper gown, hung up
like art in this cubicle, will be creased
by the patient clutching pants and shoes.

Cliff Lounge

a marram of nappy and cardigan blooms

        (the ninety-year-old
                must be ever so poorly
        blown to and fro)

on a promontory

        (look at that baby
      throwing his ball
          can you believe how strong
      he stumbles
          he pulls at things)

shells frame Queenie
as an antique

        (she seems amazed
               at our barbecue
      in a box)

a tide across the carpet
there are melanomas
on the soles of rocks

           (can she eat the cake)

gorse cushions
the blackhaired sea
nags the cliff

        (careful careful
          babies will climb
      you can't stop them
         eating dirt)

flasks of brine
the lukewarm sun
unbuttons our shirts

Divested Days

The sun earmarks the moment before
coats fly out like quilted moths
to nibble lanes and stiles, when a glove
striped with car wheels straddles a box
of apples marked Help Yourself, and hats
are crammed into pockets and you dress
paperily before the itch of lanolin
brands wrists and waist with wool. Walkwood,
Headless Cross. A pulse of lichen flashes
green, an ankle running along the fence.
The sign has been burned: Callow Hill.
A skull of a car, abandoned.

Cheval de Frise

It was because she wasn't overlooked
because our street is one-side only
and opposite the full length of our houses
there's a wall, it's *because* no view,
that my neighbour hung a balcony
across her upper storey. The first

stand-out. They multiplied, a gallery
to step onto, raising knees high
through windows, or through French doors.
They float us in the air like life jackets
but, even so, we grip the canvas scaffold
of deckchairs when we set down mugs

on armrests, balance sunglasses
on the rims of flower pots, in order
to stare at lichens, mosses, water stains
and those ancient regular naked boles
of parasite, we've learned, an *epiphyte*
that escalades over the coping, invisibly

leaving behind the glass and iron spikes.
Our mews is mentioned in the Area Guide
so tourists occasionally come to see
'*the cagey prominences*'! But for us,
whoever owns it, whatsoever it blinds –
grass pissing seeds inside dumped factories,

elder saplings cracking through concrete,
limbless petrol pumps, padlocked shafts –
however chafed with particulates,
it is that bent-shouldered, standing wall
that makes our heritage. What blank thing
do you look at without altering?

Lift

Insects of wet skated down
inside my shirt. Hooded, muddied people
pushed past us wrapped in a creosote odour
of damp coat. My mother, who would sandbag
our house against fire but never flood,
didn't worry about rain. My father
rolled out stories of smoke jumpers diving
skylines of fire. They both swept tapers
from under pine trees. Cousins, macabre
with hair-grease, slid up the razed clay
to greet us. Once inside uncurtained
glass, we'd all gaze at the high rise flats,
their drapes, balconies, those little cat baskets
of iron, and watch the long shivering
thin ropes of a lift tremble and hold.

Glass Harmonica

To avoid talking, because all afternoon
we chatted at the iron ends of her bed

and she rests, dying, we play
with wet fingers the glass harmonica.

Six rims hum. She doesn't eat,
hasn't spoken for weeks, lying upstairs.

Our boiled potatoes gleam, bald, exquisite,
through champagne flutes to toast her birthday.

The crystal sings her down. She strokes the door
open, thin as a lip, bare toes

like drops of water on red kitchen tiles.
Breath bird scratching at a border.

Untitled

Single bed. Tall brown lidded
    bin with a foot-press handle.
        White porcelain sink. Deluxe
soap dispenser. Alcohol hand rub.

Orange rubber-tiled floor. Uncontrollable
    curtain reacting over and over
        to a breeze sniping in through
the horizontal slit of an open window.

A high shelf on wheels covered with jugs,
    tiny pink square sponges on sticks,
        cc measures, a blank menu
choice dated tomorrow, Vaseline,

Sou Son body crème, Chanel perfume spray,
    a stack of disposable grey papier-mâché
        hats to vomit into, a half-moon
insert for the chin cut out.

Fennel

Zesting all over my front garden, how her fennel clings

to the removal men. As if it is interested

in boxes. In my leaving today. I haven't trimmed it.

It fixes on my shoulder. Neither have I named the house,

this semi, as she begged me to, Fennel Cottage.

The new owners may scrape the taste of my house

off its surface. But her fennel seeds cranny in fissures

and plan a dynasty of yellow tang.

Forthcoming Titles

Above the Body

He said he was fed up
with slow surgery nurses
letting him down and could she
get lost in whichever of the million
universes her expertise dictated, now
the procedure was nearly over, and accept
anaesthetists have problems with intubation.

Her recent intensive
Perception of Perceptions
Day suggested it is the same
consciousness that gets out at
death as gets in between procedure
and opinion but her interior comment
was *fart face* as she said: 'Dying is only

a sleep with friends.
That why-me attitude is
what makes you so unreal.
I am glad of a million universes.'
'So comfort is not just for patients,'
he said. 'You'd nurse black holes, stars
that die, would you, slow them down as they

enter death? Why not
rerun everything especially
what has happened in the last
five minutes of their life when they
were stretched like my patience till they
were ribbon in space? Will you be at all
fazed when you are haunted by a ribbon?'

She said 'The white hole
extruding ribbon is the next
universe, where have you been,
wake up *there* and consciousness
is as good as *here*, a million universes
better given the best that you can offer is
sedation.' 'How intoxicating to hear after a day

of bladder repairs,' he said,
'since, despite our daily holing
of flesh, you intrigue me. You're not
yet a past universe but deep, a hidden
vein. Would you be interested in a week-
end boning up on Reagent Specificities or How
Assay Methods Significantly Vary Concentration?'

Fool's Seal

He thinks: An elephant seal. It swims
towards him, trumpets from the Pacific –
becomes kelp. Images
of weed. He throws the camera down.

Though she'd never know that dark
glint wasn't a Grey, a Harbour,
a Hawaiian monk, makes
plastic, ice-cream, cold things.

Empty Shells

nut, comb, tusk, mail, sea
ear, slit, blue-rayed limpet

Sand slid over your legs
to see each side. Waves thickened
ash into cream. The wind
asked about you: is this the innard

wedge, coin, oval piddock,
trough, blunt telling, smooth Venus

of a species, its tiny gut,
or a piece of its heart or brain?
The rain demanded a lick.
Don't you wish you had stayed

Kelly, auger, nerite,
triangular Astarte

on the boardwalk, gripping a rail?
The moon calls to the sun
as it pulls the tide today: Look,
the twins are separate.

spiny cockle, prickly cockle, heart
urchin, blunt gaper

Eagle Stone

This will hurt you
heart:
ingoring cut.
You pace
the tasks of blade,
flesh-bored like I am.
Slash slash
pause.
Ignore lost blood.
Wave it on.
Lesions
soon welt over.
Shut down
the aetiology
of scar.
It's my skin,
my thin iron,
I dig through
toward the loose
nucleus,
eagle stone,
sawing the curt
red edge
of words.

Note: The eagle stone, fabled to be found in the eagle's nest, is a hollow
nodule of argillaceous oxide of iron. It has a loose nucleus.

77A

The double decker sways against the branches
of Millbank. I race with it. The ad
along the back says *Catch the Sun* Instead.

It lurches past me, suddenly brakes. Accelerates,
clearing a space to trumpet through. I cling
almost onto its end when it hangs deep

into the corner of Vauxhall Bridge and stumbles,
swerves across my path as I fly sideways.
So dissimilar, a bus, a bike.

it seems they can't collide. I slide off
sheer red cliff and smack the road. Shout:
You ran me down. It stops at the light. I palm

its side, limping, for a handhold, crawl
under its windscreen. A small white notice:
YOU could drive this 77A

to Westminster, Vauxhall, Wandsworth.
The driver's arm on the sill is wet with sweat.
Passengers gaze. I've lamed their elephant.

Blind

Two men enter my carriage.
Both are blind, sit close,
riding the rush hour.

Like a glass shoe,
the blind men try
each other.

I won't come, one says,
and see you inside.
You shouldn't have said those things.

They carry sticks.
The younger extends his,
strokes the bent, bald head.

He gets off. The older
peers, it looks like,
through the carriage window.

The Purchase of Rhythm

A tiler who is straddling the skylight
pulls himself to standing, clasps the roof,
inches his right foot to the top rung
of a red painted ladder, climbs down,
picks up a large slate, reclimbs.

The other carries a ridge tile up,
sits, shoulders making a spirit level
for the line of the loft. His collar strings
swing loose. Wind kneads plastic
covering the window hole. Puts away

yellow gloves, takes a wooden measure
from his full pocket, marks, removes
the ridge tile, shifts back, turns,
red hair against grey, eases down,
his legs scissoring as Tubalcain

taps in rivets with a taptap
taptap taptap, binary music
louder than the saw. A black bucket
hangs off the scaffolding, white
with cement. Jubal listens, stares

at the new rhetoric of the roof.
Bends over, slides a recut tile
along to cap a joint, broods on the kinked
loft ridge next door, crawls down, refiles,
retries. His hands carry as smoothly

through wet air as his fat-toed boots
slip down sheer slope. Every few feet,
stops against the weight of the wind,
his head angled against its form. Now
the ridger surveys the purchase of each piece

for the ground's deadline. A woman
below flashes a camera upwards.
The tilers don't pause. Neither faces
the other now nor smiles though theirs
is a slow smile, held as long as a step.

The Museum of Making Up

The wandering account executive,
  her hands full of coffee, client proofs,
    touches the Heisenberg '45
      for luck.
Oak, studded with brass, roped off,
  it sits so low, men tower over it.

The colour adjusters match flesh tones
  with tubes as Drainage Choice roars
    through a cathedral of rollers
      into print
and forty thousand pages an hour
  are stapled. Then the 2000 stops.

Quality checkers take out ear plugs.
  Vats of orange wait. The platemaker
    cuts a perfect plate to replace
      his mistake
surrounded by film. She whispers, 'Digital?'
  Ink stinks in the felt like bergamot.

New Bloom Country

At four in the morning, during the eighth bottle of Pinot Grigio,
three of us wander, guessing the date and origin of outstanding
objects.

Two risk-takers with a reflector, two sisters and an ex-husband,
two vegetarians, one vegan. The two academics tease the poet.
Two partners, a single woman.

Driving licence – California 2000. Lime green Vitali ash tray –
Fiesole 1968. Concert programme (Beethoven) – easy, Amsterdam
1999. Antique card game, Sorry – Huddersfield 1934.

The origin of the orchid beats us, its cream skin stippled with
strawberry, white wings outstretched, legs up, colour sucked into
the centre. We stumble between study and corridor, too late to
go home for two of us.

Mondays at Cineworld

'Home of lost causes, and forsaken beliefs,
and unpopular names, and impossible loyalties!'
        Matthew Arnold

It's a first-wife thing. Margaret parts
the curtains, waves. My second wife,
she knows I hunt a balloon caught

in a bare tree. If I died, there'd be
this habit binding Margaret – if she cared
to stammer out a script mid-row

when someone pushed past. Like a score
we splinter, me called on, her (which
her, I leave to you), impossibly loyal.

The Rarity of Funeral Parlours

On access day, she buzzes round her mother,
crossing off their differences of opinion.
Packs a penny-handle bag. Clings,
inside the wardrobe, to her clothes, her back
against raw wood. In the conservatory,
under the blue tinted perspex roof,

her separated father waits
to take her shopping. Leaves like glittering
birds flap above the alleyway.
There's not one single death shop
in the mall, she says to her father, spookily
good-looking in the unexpected sun.

He points out there's more to do than die
on the High Street also. Back home,
body warmers and cropped tops smell
garlicky, damp, as where pine hedges
a meadow carpeted with crushed stems.

Cuckoo Clock

A shadow twin was born　　　　when he remarried
– the permanent newness of his first

wife's death.　　　　The new wife
was living glitter, holly trees

papered in gold.　　　　In moments of insight,
a husband needs to

describe, for example, how the other　helped him to
let a pig escape an abattoir

or some such. He wasn't accused of　too many Guinnesses,
keeping quiet over the cuckoo clock,

whose doors stuck, bought　　　　at the local beauty spot,
on the day they'd found the shadow;

irrelevant, she didn't want that,　annexed in an odd country,
the new wife would not have it.

Pilgrim

Wales is visible down Coursing Batch
if it isn't misty when you lean
far out from Bishop Whittaker's room
in the George and Pilgrims. Pulling back
inside the window, I think of the night
before he was hung, drawn and quartered.
That sliver of light round the door, the groan
of oak boards, would have maddened him.

Nothing creaks inside my house on the junction.
The windows lie in plastic frames without
a struggle. But instead of another country
en suite, there is a hair salon where women
flower in foil-wrapped roots and once a lorry
printed its ton of thumb on the facade.

Verge

A flash of light rotates behind the workers
in yellow jackets and orange trousers.
They wave on a patient queue of cars.

White lines smoke off from verges
we have driven so tightly for years.
Covered in soot, the men bite away

old markings ready for a new language.
Now, the grey road is an open horizon,
a British winter sky, nothing higher

than cloud, distance falling back towards us,
reaching this trackless path, our limit.

Nostalgia

Hissing, calling, bead-makers and text-merchants
on Amen Corner traded prayers with Bread Street
though that naked boy, marking the highest ground
in London, was just a soundless tile in Panyer Alley.
He should have been an embryo of my ear to the past,
an otocyst, or rising the loaves of sixteen-eighty
but all I could hear was trivial history till I saw
how a flying buttress determines fissures in moonlight.

Ill Wind
Hamlet, act 1, scene 3

Not only was Polonius wrong – a loan
oft loses both itself and friend – you get

double the business, says the Little Book
of Wisdom, which is why I lent my silver

Alfa – for the apparel oft proclaims
the man – to a woman whose kid died, driving

her car and she hadn't felt that bad ever –
soul in hoops of steel – of course she needed

handouts from the heart – and where a broker's
a friend, he's stayed for – but he was murdered after.

Othello's Apnoea

You're on your back, mouth
a small hole, apple-
stuck neck, duvet
slipped to your hip –

so who makes you call
*that can't be, I must
have, why, come on then,*
who makes you call

when I saw your own
throat wouldn't buck
or even snort one breath
past your uvula?

1816

In peace, the lieutenant longs for the old beacons.
How will he read the terrible messages,
however huge, if fog hangs round the flaps
as they open and close on shutter frames?

How can he spell out *attack* while mist makes
a second alphabet? Fires used to burn
through haze: one bonfire, a French approach,
two, really coming, four blazing bales,

a great force. He dreams of arms swinging
against thick air amongst steaming words,
while the shutter soldiers of Cabbage Hill,
Putney and Portsmouth tidy their hammocks.

Spin

The window-dresser forgets bodies, steels pleats, pins cloth, a
charcoal that ticks with blue and red, gathers softness in a stiff
weave as if he were voiding grey sky of cloud to make draperies
that could float inside basilica domes.

He poises stuff in movements Gap and Next ignore.

Above him, a sign: shears open,

points up. Who reads his window? In the absence

of graphics and words, models and ready-mades, we still see the
shapes of men, kicked, spun, a regiment of uncut rolls tumbling
onto a battlefield, unmeasured.

Along this stretch of closures, his window is lit.

Mail hangs in adjacent doors.

Like Christmas, the mall is coming.

Airfish

Hooded in a hazel coracle
waterproofed with pitch and tar, between

tin mine and slate quarry – abandoned –

he rests.

The stream opens
as if a fish leaps. Closes,

the depth clear to sand. Cracks open,
closes

again, empty again. Life
after life escapes

like livelihoods in front
of a branch webbed into net with debris.

Fail Safe

Why do I never reassure myself that there is a pile of sand
mixed with small rods under a claw of bullet-headed
iron on a thick steel pole, greased with dirty
yellow tallow thus to run back smoothly,
under impact, into a big blue bolted
sheath? When rails taper to
expiry in a tunnel, is it so
hopeless?

One-way System

In a landscape of spectacular wrappers,
huge electric adverts promise transport
beyond Capitol Studios, Ace Wine,
the marble and slate yard, and a man,
stooped, unshaven, grey hair, stands

at the bus-stop – an advert for a passenger,
full of expectation – as if the bus,
parked, empty of a driver, is ready
to move to the boarding point, open
its doors, take us. We hang back.

We don't assume the 77A
will recognise its queue, won't smile
towards it but face the Huguenot houses,
restored refugees. They are solicitors'
offices, now, a listed Site of Hope.

Learner

We used to hear him practise all the time,
midwifery of music. Two men
grappled the bulk of his piano down
three flights. Wooden veneer splintered.

To me.
Back.
Tricky.
Bit of a corner.
Easy.
Easy.
Hold it.
Nicely.
Now.

There was a bumping down of delicate sounds.
A delivery of loss out of rehearsal.

Forthcoming Titles

untitled
words selected randomly each day from an original brief to create
a wallhung definition of death
Titled:
Definition of Death

untitled
medical plates of the dead brain collected from assorted hospital
archives
Titled:
Dead Head Shots, Interior

untitled
plaster casts of family and neighbours in appropriate shades,
hung as domestic decorations. Marie has her eyes open.
Titled:
Memento Marie

untitled
street names which refer to, imply, name or euphemise the notion
of death
Titled:
Short Cuts

untitled
photographic studies of flesh lit to illuminate death blows
Titled:
Shiners

untitled
technologically-inspired sadomasochistic fetishes which have
been implicated in a death, each with linked tabloid headline
Titled:
Thumbscrew to Palmtop

untitled
constant-play video recording of the artist in conversation,
constructed wholly of phrases used by dying celebrities, with an
unnamed friend
Titled:
I Shall Make an Attempt to Fill the Void

Lightning Source UK Ltd.
Milton Keynes UK
UKOW03f2206190514

231962UK00001B/26/A

9 781905 700189